CONTENTS

Before You Begin   7

Some Useful Bible Words   9

Dec 1st: God's Plan for Christmas   11

Dec 2nd: Like the Stars in the Sky   14

Dec 3rd: A Promised Child   17

Dec 4th: A Stairway to God   20

Dec 5th: The Only Truly Good Person   23

Dec 6th: The Passover Lamb   26

Dec 7th: Life-Giving Bread   29

Dec 8th: God's True Tent   32

Dec 9th: Ruth's Son's Son's Son's … Son   35

Dec 10th: The Forever King   38

Dec 11th: The King Who Understands Us   41

Dec 12th: Born to Die   44

Dec 13th: God with Us   47

Dec 14th: Mary's Child   50

Dec 15th: True Happiness   53

Dec 16th: We Live for Jesus   56

Dec 17th: Preparing the Path   59

Dec 18th: The Real Jesus   62

Dec 19th: The Angel's Message for All   65

Dec 20th: The Best Words Ever   68

Dec 21st: Simeon Sees His Savior   71

Dec 22nd: God Hears Us   74

Dec 23rd: The Truth about Jesus   77

Dec 24th: Jesus Came to Win   80

Dec 25th: A Jesus Christmas   83

Extra Journaling Space   88

BEFORE YOU BEGIN

These devotions are ideal for all ages. They are about faith—trusting Jesus, not your own goodness. They are about repentance—living for Jesus, not yourself. They are for children who already believe and for those who do not yet believe in Jesus. We all need encouragement all the time to believe Jesus's truth.

Prepare your own heart before you lead your family or others in *A Jesus Christmas*. Ask your heavenly Father to guide you. Ask for insight about what questions to ask and how to promote discussion. Pray for God to give you a daily desire to make Jesus the focus of this Christmas.

THE DAILY PATTERN
Each day has four parts: Explore, Explain, Engage, and Enter in. These are followed by a wonderful true statement about Jesus and some family journaling space.

EXPLORE
Reading the Bible passage together is the key activity. The Bible will connect these true stories to show us God's plan for sending Jesus. His big picture will come into view as you start to see these themes emerge:

- God's plan for sending Jesus started in the Garden of Eden.

- Satan (the devil) was seen in the garden as a serpent/snake. Adam and Eve listened to the serpent's lie. Their sin broke everything in God's perfect world.

- Instead of running to God, we all run from him.

- God loves us more than we know. He promised to send his Son, Jesus, to crush the serpent and destroy evil.

- God planned for Jesus to come through the family line of Abraham, Isaac, Jacob, Ruth, and David.

- The serpent tells many lies but Jesus always tells the truth.

- Jesus lived and died for us to free us from the serpent's lies so that we can come to God as our Father.

- All who receive the gift of Jesus are God's children and will live with him forever.

EXPLAIN

Each day three things are highlighted: God's plan for Jesus, the serpent's lies, and Jesus's truth. Try to answer your child's questions but don't get bogged down in details. Assure everyone that as they learn more about Jesus, the truths will start to connect.

ENGAGE

There are two Engage questions for older children. The first helps children discover how truth intersects with their lives. The second question stimulates deeper discussion.

Each Engage question also has a simpler version after it. This is ideal for younger children or those with less Bible knowledge. The older and younger questions are marked as shown below:

 For older children    For younger children

Be prepared to get the conversation going. Ask God for willingness to talk about times when you are tempted to sin. Pray that you will respond to your kids with understanding and not in a judgmental tone. As your family responds honestly to God's word and Spirit, they will begin to treasure the truth of Jesus.

ENTER IN

This short prayer is a springboard for your response to whatever God shows you about himself, Jesus, and yourself. The journal notes you make will continue to remind you of how God has used his Spirit and his word to work eternal miracles in your family.

JESUS IS...

These "Jesus is…" statements will help your family to remember that Christmas is about Jesus. Some have been decorated for you, though your child may want to add extra stars and patterns. Others have letter outlines for your child to color in.

FAMILY JOURNALING SPACE

This is a place to respond to what God has shown you. You might want to write down what you have learned, draw a picture, list things to thank God for, draw how your face looks when you think about Jesus, or use this space for any other way you want to respond to God. There is some extra journaling space at the back of the book for any days when you have an idea that needs more room.

ANSWERS

If you would find it helpful, you can download an answer sheet to all of the Explore and Engage questions from **www.thegoodbook.com/ajc-answers.pdf**

TIPS FOR SUCCESS

Be brief. Be real. Be consistent.

SOME USEFUL BIBLE WORDS

AMEN: This Hebrew word means "I agree." It is a way of joining in with someone's prayer.

BIBLE / SCRIPTURE / GOD'S BOOK: Although the Bible was written by about 40 people, God made sure that they wrote exactly what he wanted them to write. God speaks to us through the Bible, and what he says in the Bible is always true.

CHRISTMAS: We don't know exactly when Jesus was born, but December 25th was chosen as a day to celebrate Christmas—the birth of Jesus Christ.

FULFILLED: When one of God's promises is fulfilled, it means that he has done exactly what he promised to do. When Jesus was born at the very first Christmas, he fulfilled many of God's promises.

ISRAEL / ISRAELITES / GOD'S CHILDREN: God promised Abraham that his family would be so huge that counting them would be like trying to count all of the stars. This family were God's people, often known as the Israelites or simply Israel. God promised that his rescuing King would come from this family.

MERCY: Mercy is when God doesn't treat us in the way we deserve. Instead God shows us grace, which is his huge kindness to people who don't deserve it.

MESSIAH / CHRIST: "Messiah" is a Hebrew word. The same word in Greek is "Christ." They both mean "the anointed one." When someone became king, they were anointed with oil. The names Messiah and Christ tell us that Jesus is God's chosen King.

SERPENT: In the Garden of Eden, Satan (the devil) was seen as a serpent/snake.

SIN / SINFUL: When we sin, we do what **we** want instead of what **God** wants. In our hearts we believe the lies of the serpent more than we believe God. Jesus came to rescue us from the problem of sin.

THE CROSS: Jesus's enemies killed him by nailing him to a cross and leaving him there to die. But it was God who had already planned that Jesus would die. As Jesus died on the cross, he took all the punishment for our sin, so that everyone who trusts in Jesus can be forgiven.

DECEMBER 1ST
GOD'S PLAN FOR CHRISTMAS

EXPLORE

Read Genesis 3 v 1-5 and 14-15

What lie did the serpent tell Adam and Eve? (verses 4-5)

_____

_____

_____

What did God tell the serpent? (verses 14-15)

_____

_____

_____

EXPLAIN

God's plan for the first Christmas starts right at the beginning of the Bible. God built a beautiful garden for Adam and Eve's home. He talked with them like best friends talk, and gave them lots of delicious fruit to eat. God loved Adam and Eve so much that he warned them not to eat the fruit of one tree. They would die if they ate that fruit.

But a serpent in the garden (who was really Satan) told them God had lied. The serpent said they couldn't trust what God said. Was the serpent telling the truth? No! God _always_ speaks what is true. Sadly, Adam and Eve believed the serpent and ate the fruit. Now weeds grow and God's creatures die. Worse yet, the terrible lie of the serpent lives on in every human heart. Instead of running to God, we run from him.

God loved Adam and Eve so much more than they thought. Adam's and Eve's sin broke everything. But God made the best-ever promise! **God promised to send someone to crush the serpent and destroy evil.** That someone is Jesus.

ENGAGE

⭐ Why do we run away from God instead of to him?

_____

_____

_____

⭐ Ever since Adam and Eve believed the serpent, what lives in our hearts?

_____

_____

_____

⭐ What makes God's promise of Jesus the very best promise ever?

_____

_____

_____

⭐ What promise did God give to Adam and Eve and us all?

_____

_____

_____

ENTER IN

God, you are our good Father. Thank you for your promise to send Jesus. We want to learn what it means to run to you and stop running from you. Help us know you and love you more this Christmas and always. Amen.

JESUS IS GOD'S
PROMISE

FAMILY JOURNALING SPACE

IDEAS: Write "JESUS" in big letters and color in;
or write your own prayer; or something else…

DECEMBER 2ND
LIKE THE STARS IN THE SKY

EXPLORE

Read Genesis 15 v 1-6

What did God promise Abram? (verses 4-5)

How did Abram respond to God's promise? (verse 6)

EXPLAIN

Christmas is God's answer to our biggest problem. God promised to send Jesus to rescue us from the serpent's terrible lie in our hearts. But *how* would God send Jesus?

God told a man named Abram, "Do not be afraid. I am your great reward." God promised him a son. Did Abram hear this right? He and his wife, Sarai, were too old to have a baby. Then God told him something even more amazing: "Look up into the night sky and count the stars." Abram would have as many children as there are stars. And from Abram's son's son's son's … son the Rescuer would come.

Abram believed God. He did not listen to the serpent's lie that says, "You have to see it *before* you can believe it." The truth is, we see the truth when we believe in Jesus. God gives us hearts that can see. Jesus is the Rescuer—who lived all his perfect life for us. And Jesus died for every wrong thing we do. **Jesus rescues everyone who believes in him.**

ENGAGE

Why is believing the truth about Jesus a good thing? What does this mean for you?

_____

_____

_____

Why do we need Jesus to rescue us?

_____

_____

What would you say to someone who asked, "Why do we need Jesus?"

_____

_____

_____

Who does Jesus rescue?

_____

_____

ENTER IN

Father God, you are powerful. Thank you for making it possible for Abram to believe you and your promise to him. Please take away our unbelief. Give us new hearts to believe you and your promise of Jesus. Amen.

DID YOU KNOW? *God gave new names to Abram and Sarai. When we read about them tomorrow, they will be called Abraham and Sarah.*

BARBARA REAOCH

☆ ☆ ☆
JESUS IS OUR
RESCUER
☆ ☆ ☆

FAMILY JOURNALING SPACE

IDEAS: Draw lots and lots of stars; or write why Jesus is the greatest Rescuer of all; or something else…

❦ DECEMBER 3ʳᵈ ❦
A PROMISED CHILD

EXPLORE

Read Genesis 21 v 1-6

What did God give to Abraham and Sarah, just as he promised? (verses 1-2)

_____

_____

_____

How did Sarah react to having a son? (verse 6)

_____

_____

_____

EXPLAIN

Christmas is God's way of saying, "I always keep my promises." God promised to make Abraham the father of many children. Best of all, one of his son's son's son's ... sons would be Jesus! But when no son was born, the terrible lie of the serpent made him wonder, "How can I be sure God will keep his promise?"

When Sarah heard God's promise to give her a child, she laughed (Genesis 18 v 12). After all, what does a pregnant 90-year-old look like?! But, nine months later, Sarah gave birth to a baby boy. They named him _Isaac_, which means "son of laughter." Sarah laughed again, this time from a heart of joy.

Christmas tells us that Jesus is God's "YES" to all of his promises. When God came out of heaven, in Jesus, he proved that all of his promises are true. Jesus's joy fills our hearts when we believe in him. The joy of a Christmas gift lasts only a short time. But the joy Jesus puts in our hearts lasts forever. **Jesus is real joy!**

ENGAGE

For every day to seem like Christmas, we would need gifts and special treats every day. Why does the joy from a Christmas gift last only a short time?

_____

_____

_____

How do we know God always keeps his promises?

_____

_____

_____

The lasting joy we all really want comes from Jesus. Have you told him, "Jesus, I trust you as my Rescuer; you alone can give me a new heart and a new life with you forever"?

_____

_____

_____

How long does the joy that Jesus gives us last?

_____

_____

_____

ENTER IN

God, you are the Promise-Keeper. You have the power to keep all your promises. Please give us the forever joy of trusting Jesus as our Rescuer. Amen.

JESUS IS JOY!

FAMILY
JOURNALING
SPACE

IDEAS: Draw Abraham and Sarah with baby Isaac; or list gifts from God that make you happy; or something else…

DECEMBER 4TH
A STAIRWAY TO GOD

EXPLORE

Read Genesis 28 v 10-17

What did Jacob see in his dream? (verse 12)

_____

_____

_____

What did God promise Jacob? (verses 13-15)

_____

_____

_____

EXPLAIN

God's plan for the first Christmas included an unlikely guy named Jacob. Abraham's grandsons, Jacob and Esau, were twins. Jacob tricked his brother and lied to his father, Isaac. Jacob messed up a lot and knew his father loved Esau more. But God chose Jacob. God would send Jesus to bless the world through Jacob's family.

The terrible lie of the serpent whispers, "You haven't kept your promises to God—how will he keep his promise to you?" The truth is, Jesus came to rescue promise-breakers like Jacob. In a dream, God showed Jacob a stairway with angels going up and down from heaven to earth. God came to Jacob. Jacob did not have to climb the stairway to God.

Christmas tells us that Jesus **is** the Stairway (John 1 v 51). God didn't send Jesus to help us be strong enough to climb up to him. God loves us so much that Jesus came down to get us. God's rescue plan is better than we could ever dream. We don't have to rescue ourselves... **Jesus takes us to God.**

ENGAGE

⭐ How is Jesus the Stairway to God?

_____

_____

_____

⭐ Who is the Stairway to God?

_____

_____

⭐ People say that Santa's gifts depend on how you answer the question, "Have you been good this year?" The Bible asks a totally different question: "Have you trusted in Jesus (not in your own goodness)?" Have you received God's gift of Jesus and given him your love and life?

_____

_____

_____

⭐ What is God's rescue plan?

_____

_____

_____

ENTER IN

Father God, you are always right and just. We're amazed that you know we mess up and yet you love us. Thank you for sending Jesus to be strong for us. Help us rest in your great love. Amen.

☆ ☆ ☆
JESUS IS THE
STAIRWAY
☆ ☆ ☆

FAMILY JOURNALING SPACE

IDEAS: Draw angels on a stairway; or write a prayer thanking God for loving us when we mess up; or something else…

❦ DECEMBER 5ᵀᴴ ❦
THE ONLY TRULY GOOD PERSON

EXPLORE

Read Exodus 3 v 4-10

Why did Moses need to take off his sandals? (verses 5-6)

_____

_____

_____

Why was God sending Moses to Egypt? (verses 8-10)

_____

_____

_____

EXPLAIN

Moses was part of God's plan for the first Christmas. The family of Abraham, Isaac and Jacob grew into a very big family called Israel. But something was terribly wrong. God's people—often called God's children—were slaves! They lived far away in a place called Egypt. God sent Moses to lead his people. Moses loved God and was a good person. Moses would rescue God's children from slavery. But he could not crush the head of the serpent.

The serpent whispers, "Any good person could rescue you." The truth is, no matter how good or wise, all teachers and leaders are sinful. Jesus is the only truly good Teacher and Leader. The serpent tempted Jesus, but Jesus won every fight against sin. Only Jesus never sinned, so only Jesus can rescue us.

Christmas tells us that Jesus is much more than a good person—he is fully God and fully human. Only Jesus can bring us to God. God's Book, the Bible, says, "Jesus has been found worthy of greater honor than Moses, just as the builder of a house has greater honor than the house itself" (Hebrews 3 v 3). **Jesus is our only way to God.**

ENGAGE

⭐ Why is Jesus the only one who can rescue us?

⭐ Who is the only one that can rescue us?

⭐ Christmas is mostly fun, but problems happen. When you speak mean words and you sin, how can Jesus be your Rescuer? (Adults, share honestly about your own need, to get the discussion going.)

⭐ How is Jesus different from every other good person?

ENTER IN

Father God, you have a big plan for your people. Jesus, help us remember how powerful you are. Please use your perfect strength to rescue us from impatience and worry. We want you to be at the center of this Christmas and not us. Amen.

JESUS NEVER SINNED

FAMILY
JOURNALING
SPACE

IDEAS: Draw the burning bush (Exodus 3 v 2); or copy God's name from Exodus 3 v 6; or something else…

 DECEMBER 6TH
THE PASSOVER LAMB

EXPLORE

Read Exodus 12 v 21-27

The leaders of Israel were also called elders. What instructions did Moses give to them? (verses 21-23)

What did God's people tell their children about Passover? (verses 26-27)

EXPLAIN

The miracle of Christmas was coming. But God's people were still slaves in Egypt. Had God forgotten them? No! To help them wait for the first Christmas, God gave them pictures of what Jesus would be like. The first picture was the Passover lamb (1 Corinthians 5 v 7). Jesus the Lamb was coming.

God warned the Egyptians how bad sin is. But they listened to the serpent whisper, "God won't really punish anyone." The truth is, sin hurts us and everyone. So God's love for all people means he must punish sin. God lovingly planned a way to punish evil and forgive his children at the same time. God punished evil in all of Egypt. But the lamb's blood on the door-frames kept his people safe inside their houses.

Christmas tells us Jesus is the Lamb (John 1 v 29). Jesus never sinned, but he took the punishment for sin that we deserve. When Jesus hung on the cross, his body was broken and his blood poured out, to keep us safe with God. God's greatest gift to you is his only Son. **Jesus rescues us from God's punishment for sin.**

ENGAGE

★ Why is it good to see how bad sin is?

★ The Bible calls Jesus the Lamb. Why?

★ Imagine this: When a fire came, a mother bird covered her chicks with her body to keep them safe. She died but the fire did not touch the chicks. Punishment for sin will be like a deadly fire. How does knowing Jesus as your Passover Lamb help you know you are safe from sin's punishment?

★ What is God's plan to punish evil and forgive his people at the same time?

ENTER IN

Father God, you are right and just. Your warnings come from your heart of love. Please help us replace the lies that we've believed about sin with your truth. Thank you for sending Jesus to be our Passover Lamb. Amen.

✩ ☆ ✩
JESUS IS THE
LAMB OF GOD
✩ ☆ ✩

FAMILY
JOURNALING
SPACE

IDEAS: Draw a door-frame and color the top and sides red; or write a prayer thanking Jesus for being our Passover Lamb; or something else…

DECEMBER 7TH
LIFE-GIVING BREAD

EXPLORE

Read Exodus 16 v 1-5 and 31

Why did the people grumble? (verses 1-3)

_____

_____

_____

What did the people call the bread God gave them to eat? (verse 31)

_____

_____

EXPLAIN

How hard it was to wait for the first Christmas! On the long walk to their new home, God gave his children a second picture of Jesus—manna, the special bread with which he fed them. Their tummies were full but their hearts didn't see the picture of Jesus. All they could think about was the food they missed and how hard this new life was.

The serpent's terrible lie asks, "Is life with God really better than life without him?" The truth is, life with God is the only way to true happiness. God made us for himself. We may hunger for money, friends, talents, looking good and being smart. but only God fills our hearts and truly satisfies. Jesus, the Bread of Life, fills us up with his life.

Christmas tells us that Jesus is the true Manna (John 6 v 31-35). Bread fills our stomachs, but Jesus fills our hearts. The taste of Jesus in your heart is so much sweeter than freshly baked bread in your mouth. **Jesus fills our hearts with his life.**

ENGAGE

How is Jesus the only way to true happiness?

_____

_____

_____

Why is Jesus the Bread of life?

_____

_____

_____

What kind of hunger do you see in the lives of your friends? Now, be honest with yourself—what hunger is in your life? (Adults, talk about ways you hunger for lesser things than Jesus, to encourage open sharing.)

_____

_____

_____

When is a person truly happy?

_____

_____

_____

ENTER IN

Father God, you are faithful. Help us see that you meet our needs better than everything else we love so much. Thank you for the promise of Jesus. As we read your Book and pray today, help us taste the sweetness of Jesus. Amen.

JESUS IS THE BREAD OF LIFE

FAMILY JOURNALING SPACE

IDEAS: Draw what you think manna looked like; or write how Jesus is like bread; or something else…

DECEMBER 8TH
GOD'S TRUE TENT

EXPLORE

Read Exodus 25 v 1-9

Why did God want the people to build a tabernacle (big tent)? (verse 8)

How did the people know what to build? (verse 9)

EXPLAIN

Why was the first Christmas taking so long? On the long walk to their new home, God gave his children a third picture of Jesus. God loved his children so much that he made his home right in the middle of their neighborhood. God's big, beautiful tent was his new home.

Adam and Eve had once lived with God. They walked and talked with God as best friends do. But after Adam and Eve believed the serpent's lie, they ran and hid from God. Now the serpent whispers, "God lives so far away. Does he really love you?" The truth is God has always loved us so much more than we think. He showed his love by sending Jesus. Jesus is God's true Tent (John 1 v 14).

Christmas tells us that Jesus came to make his home in our hearts. Jesus is so close to his people that he even hears what they think. And he sees everything. Not even a hair falls from your head unless it is in his good plan for you. **Jesus came to make your heart his home.**

ENGAGE

⭐ What does it mean to you that God loves you so much that he wants you to be close to him?

_____

_____

_____

⭐ Who is God's true Tent?

_____

_____

⭐ It is easy to feel lonely when you believe God lives far away. What loneliness do you see in the lives of your friends? How might God use you to help them know his love?

_____

_____

_____

⭐ Where does Jesus make his home?

_____

_____

_____

ENTER IN

Father God, thank you for your amazing love. You are not far away. You are close and you care. Jesus, please make our hearts your home. We want to know you and love you more and more. Amen.

JESUS IS GOD'S TENT

FAMILY JOURNALING SPACE

IDEAS: Draw a big tent; or draw a heart for each person in your family and write "Jesus" inside each one; or something else…

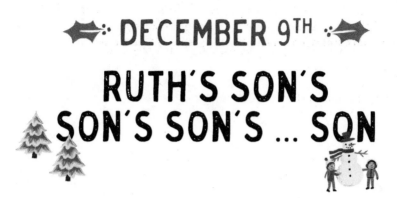

DECEMBER 9TH
RUTH'S SON'S SON'S SON'S ... SON

EXPLORE

Read Ruth 4 v 13-17

How did the women describe Naomi's daughter-in-law, Ruth? (verses 14-15)

_____

_____

_____

What was the name of Naomi's grandchild (Boaz and Ruth's son)? (verse 17)

_____

_____

EXPLAIN

Was it ever going to be Christmas? Life was scary for God's children. Everyone was hungry. That's when Naomi and her husband left their home in Bethlehem. It got worse. Naomi's husband and two sons died. Naomi was all alone except for her son's wife, Ruth. And Ruth did not yet know God. But God's plan for Christmas included Ruth.

The serpent whispers, "Only good people are in God's family." The truth is, God adopts everyone into his family who turns from the serpent's lies and trusts in Jesus. God is not ashamed to call you his child whether you belong to a good family or feel that you don't belong at all. Ruth chose to believe God.

Christmas tells us that all who trust in Jesus are God's children. Ruth's name is right there in Jesus's family tree (Matthew 1 v 5). Ruth married Boaz, a man from Abraham's family. Even more amazing, their son Obed was King David's grandfather. But most amazing of all, Ruth's son's son's son's … son was Jesus. **Anyone who turns from sin and trusts in Jesus is God's child.**

ENGAGE

⭐ Who can become a child in God's family?

_____

_____

_____

⭐ Who did Ruth choose to believe, and who was her son's son's son's … son?

_____

_____

_____

⭐ When you are in a new school or neighborhood, Christmas can be hard. Who do you know who might feel that they don't belong? How could you show them that Jesus's love includes them?

_____

_____

_____

⭐ Who does God adopt into his family?

_____

_____

_____

ENTER IN

Father God, you are so kind. Thank you for loving all people and including people of every color, nation, and tribe in your family. Please forgive us for sometimes playing favorites only with those who look like us and live like we do. Give us your heart for all people. Amen.

JESUS DOESN'T HAVE
FAVORITES

FAMILY JOURNALING SPACE

IDEAS: Draw lots of different people; or list at least ten countries and thank God that he loves people from every country; or something else...

DECEMBER 10TH
THE FOREVER KING

EXPLORE

Read 2 Samuel 7 v 8-13

What are the four things the LORD did for David? (verses 8-9)

_____

_____

_____

What did the LORD promise to build for David? (verses 11-13)

_____

_____

_____

EXPLAIN

David was a big part of God's Christmas plan. David—Boaz and Ruth's great-grandson—was a shepherd in Bethlehem. God loved David and made him king. David loved God and did many great things for him. Then, David decided to build a big, beautiful home for God.

The serpent whispers, "Do great things for God and he will love you." The truth is, God loves us not because of what we do but because of Jesus. We could never deserve God's love by what we do. God told David, "Actually, I'm going to build a house for you. Not a house of wood and stone, but a family with a son who will be a king forever." From then on, God's children knew King David's son's son's son's ... son would be God's promised forever King. That means Jesus!

Christmas tells us that Jesus is God's King who rules forever. The angel announced, "He will be great ... the Lord God will give him the throne of his father David, and he will reign ... forever; his kingdom will never end" (Luke 1 v 32-33). **Jesus is the King that God promised to send.**

ENGAGE

★ Why do some people think they need to do good things for God to love them?

_____

_____

_____

★ Who is King David's son's son's son's ... son?

_____

_____

★ If we study hard, we get good grades. If we practice hard, we get on the team. And at Christmas, some people say that if we are good, we get lots of gifts! How is God's way different?

_____

_____

_____

★ What did God build for King David?

_____

_____

ENTER IN

Father God, you are the Master Planner. You are building a kingdom for King Jesus. And you kindly used David's family in your plan. Sometimes we think that we have to earn your love. Help us to believe the truth that we are your children because of what you have done for us. Amen.

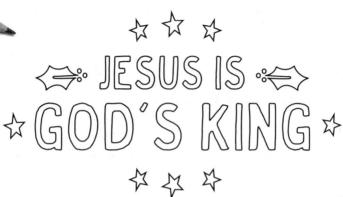

JESUS IS GOD'S KING

FAMILY JOURNALING SPACE

IDEAS: Draw a beautiful crown; or draw David's family tree (father Jesse, grandfather Obed, and great-grandparents Ruth and Boaz); or something else…

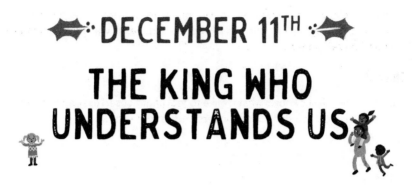 DECEMBER 11TH
THE KING WHO UNDERSTANDS US

EXPLORE

Read Isaiah 9 v 6-7

What will the child be called? (verse 6)

_____

_____

What will the child do in David's kingdom? (verse 7)

_____

_____

_____

EXPLAIN

The first Christmas was taking a long time! One king after another from King David's family ruled and then died. None of them crushed the serpent. How would King Jesus be different? What Isaiah said surprised everyone! Jesus is the Mighty God, who created the world and yet would come to us as a child. Jesus is the Everlasting Father and powerful King of the universe and yet would come as a helpless baby.

The serpent whispers, "Why did Jesus need to be a human being?" The truth is, as a human, Jesus understands us better than anyone. Jesus cried, was hungry, talked to his friends, and slept. Jesus learned to talk, read, obey, and help his parents. He understands how weak we are. Jesus went through all our temptations and yet always obeyed God. Jesus was strong for us.

Christmas tells us Jesus was born to live for us. Jesus lived all his perfect life for us. He gives strength to all who run to him for help. **Jesus was tempted in every way and never sinned.**

ENGAGE

★ Do you think Jesus knows what it's like to feel afraid or sad (Hebrews 2 v 17-18)? What else do you think Jesus understands about you?

_____

_____

_____

★ How is King Jesus different from other kings in David's family?

_____

_____

★ It helps to talk to someone who understands, so what would you like to tell Jesus?

_____

_____

_____

★ Why does Jesus understand us so well?

_____

_____

_____

ENTER IN

Father God, you are so good. Thank you for your amazing plan to send Jesus as a human. Jesus, you know us better than we know ourselves. Help us run to you for help when we are tempted. We need your strength when we are weak. Amen.

JESUS IS FULLY HUMAN

FAMILY JOURNALING SPACE

IDEAS: Draw a baby wearing a crown; or choose one name for Jesus (Isaiah 9 v 6) and write it in beautiful letters; or something else…

✦ DECEMBER 12ᵀᴴ ✦
BORN TO DIE

EXPLORE

Read Isaiah 53 v 1-6

What are four things to learn about Jesus from these verses? (verses 2-4)

_____

_____

_____

_____

Why was Jesus pierced and crushed? (verse 5)

_____

_____

EXPLAIN

King Jesus was really coming! But God's picture of a king is so different. Other kings have big houses, beautiful jewels, lots of money, and the praises of people. Most kings want to be served. But King Jesus left behind the joys of heaven and the praises of angels to come and die for us. People rejected and beat him. Jesus allowed the serpent to kill him. But this was God's rescue plan.

The serpent whispers, "Did Jesus really have to die?" The truth is, the whole world broke when Adam and Eve listened to the serpent. Only Jesus could crush the serpent and destroy evil and death. Through his death, Jesus broke the serpent's power over us.

Christmas tells us that Jesus was born to die for us. "Since the children have flesh and blood, he too shared in their humanity so that by his death he might break the power of him who holds the power of death—that is, the devil" (Hebrews 2 v 14). **Jesus died to set us free.**

ENGAGE

⭐ When Jesus died it seemed that the serpent had won. Why was it God's plan for Jesus to die?

_____

_____

_____

⭐ How is Jesus different from other kings?

_____

_____

⭐ Jesus frees us from the devil's power and gives us strength to fight against sin (John 8 v 34-36). If you are God's child, talk about a time when you were tempted to sin and Jesus gave you power to say "No." (Adults, to get the discussion going, share honestly.)

_____

_____

_____

⭐ Why did Jesus die?

_____

_____

ENTER IN

Father God, your kingdom is so different. And Jesus, you are totally different from every other king. You are loving and powerful. We want to live for you. Please give us your strength to fight against sin. When we are tempted to do what is wrong, help us remember to ask for your power to say "No." Amen.

⭐ ⭐ ⭐
JESUS IS THE
SUFFERING KING
⭐ ⭐ ⭐

FAMILY JOURNALING SPACE

IDEAS: Draw the serpent, and then cross it out because Jesus wins; or write a prayer thanking Jesus for coming to die; or something else…

DECEMBER 13TH
GOD WITH US

EXPLORE

Read Matthew 1 v 18-24

What did the angel of the Lord tell Joseph? (verses 20-21)

_____

_____

_____

What does Immanuel mean? (verse 23)

_____

_____

_____

EXPLAIN

The first Christmas was getting close! God gave Joseph the honor of bringing Jesus up as his son. But Jesus would be different from every other baby. Mary would be Jesus's mother, but Jesus is _God's_ Son.

The serpent whispers, "Isn't Jesus just a good teacher or prophet?" The truth is, Jesus is God the Son—Immanuel, God with us. With one mind and heart, the Father, Son, and Holy Spirit planned for Jesus to leave his home in heaven to come to us. Because Jesus loved us, he put on a human body, but he never sinned.

Christmas tells us that Jesus is fully God. Jesus is holy and is the way to our holy God. We can't just pretend we have clean hearts. And no matter how hard we try, we can't make ourselves good enough. God didn't send a good teacher or prophet to tell us what to do. Only Jesus could take the full and right anger of God against sin. "The Son is the image of the invisible God" (Colossians 1 v 15). **Jesus is God with us.**

ENGAGE

⭐ What did coming to rescue us cost Jesus?

_____

_____

_____

⭐ How was Jesus different from every other baby?

_____

_____

_____

⭐ What are you learning about Jesus that is making your love for him grow?

_____

_____

_____

⭐ How is Jesus different from other good teachers?

_____

_____

_____

ENTER IN

Father God, you made a way for us to stop running from you. You sent Jesus so that we can run to you with our hearts clean from sin. Jesus, thank you for leaving your amazing home in heaven. You are the only one who could open the way for us to be forgiven. Amen.

JESUS IS
FULLY GOD

FAMILY JOURNALING SPACE

IDEAS: Draw the angel; or write what it means to you that Jesus is "God with us"; or something else...

DECEMBER 14TH
MARY'S CHILD

EXPLORE

Read Luke 1 v 30-37

What are at least four things the angel told Mary about Jesus? (verses 32-33)

_____

_____

_____

_____

How did the angel answer Mary's question? (verses 35-36)

_____

_____

_____

EXPLAIN

God's plan for Christmas included a girl named Mary. But when Mary heard what the angel said, she was shocked! Mary's baby, Jesus, would be the King that God promised to rescue his people. He would not be like any other king. He would be God's Son. King Jesus would live and rule with his people forever.

The serpent lies and says, "This life is all there is." The truth is, God's people enjoy life and love with Jesus now and always. Not even death can stop this forever life. One day Jesus will wipe away all our tears.

Christmas tells us that Jesus gives us a forever life. Jesus died and the serpent thought he had won. But after three days—what a surprise! Jesus was alive again! He crushed the serpent. Jesus won victory over sin and death. Now when we close our eyes in death, we will wake up in heaven and see Jesus (John 14 v 2-3). God's children enjoy life in this world with Jesus now, one day in heaven, and then with Jesus in his kingdom forever. **Jesus is God's forever King.**

ENGAGE

★ All who turn away from sin and trust in Jesus are God's children. What could you say to a friend who is not sure they are God's child?

_____

_____

_____

★ How long will King Jesus live and rule with his children?

_____

_____

★ Jesus lived for us, died for us, and rose to life for us. One day King Jesus will come back, and then all his children will enjoy forever life with him. If you are not sure you are God's child, will you use this space to write out a prayer asking God for faith to trust Jesus?

_____

_____

_____

★ How long do God's children live?

_____

_____

ENTER IN

God, you are the loving Father of a great big family. The thought of living in your family forever in heaven is too wonderful for us to imagine. We want to be your children. Please give us faith to turn from sin and to trust Jesus as our Rescuer and King. Amen.

☆ ☆ ☆
JESUS IS KING
☆ FOREVER ☆
☆ ☆ ☆

FAMILY
JOURNALING
SPACE

IDEAS: Draw Mary and the angel; or write how you feel about being God's child; or something else…

➤ DECEMBER 15ᵀᴴ ➤
TRUE HAPPINESS

EXPLORE

Read Luke 1 v 38-45

How did Mary respond to the angel's news? (verse 38)

_____

_____

_____

What did the Holy Spirit show Elizabeth about Mary's baby? (verses 42-45)

_____

_____

_____

EXPLAIN

Christmas had almost come! Mary still had questions, but she trusted God. She said, "I am the Lord's servant. May your word to me be fulfilled." Mary and her cousin Elizabeth were both going to have babies. Elizabeth's unborn baby jumped for joy because Mary's baby was the Lord Jesus. Mary was happy that she had offered her life to God. His plan for her life was good.

The serpent's lie says, "You won't be happy unless you are in charge of your life." The truth is, God is in charge and God is good. Mary did not demand her own way. She gladly gave herself to God. True happiness is ours when we give our lives to our good God.

Christmas tells us that Jesus came to give his life to us. Now we can give our lives to him—our hands, feet, eyes, tongue, mind… and heart. Trying to get our own way in life can never make us truly happy. **True happiness comes when you give your life to Jesus.**

ENGAGE

★ Reading God's Book, praying, and obeying God are part of giving your life to Jesus. In this crazy busy time of year, what smaller joy will you put aside to spend time with God?

_____

_____

_____

★ Who knew that God's plan for her life was good?

_____

_____

★ Life with Jesus means doing whatever he wants—even when it means changing our plans. Even when it isn't fun. Even when no one else is watching! How might you use your hands, feet, eyes, tongue, mind, and heart to help someone else be truly happy today?

_____

_____

_____

★ When are we truly happy?

_____

_____

_____

ENTER IN

Father God, you are in charge and you are good. We want to know the true happiness of giving our lives to Jesus. Show us what to set aside so that we make time to talk with you and read your Book. And help us listen for the things you want us to do today. Amen.

JESUS IS LORD

FAMILY JOURNALING SPACE

IDEAS: Draw Mary and Elizabeth; or draw your hands, feet, eyes, tongue, mind, and heart; or something else…

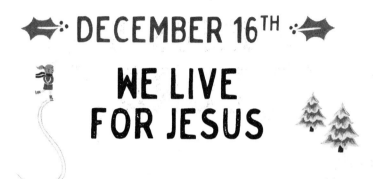

DECEMBER 16TH
WE LIVE FOR JESUS

EXPLORE

Read Luke 1 v 46-55

What did Mary say that God had done for her? (verses 48-49)

_____

_____

_____

What are at least four reasons why Mary rejoiced in God? (verses 50-55)

_____

_____

_____

EXPLAIN

Christmas was really close! How amazing! God gave Mary the gift of being the Rescuer's mother. Her heart cried out, "My soul glorifies the Lord." Now Mary knew why she was alive—to love God, enjoy him, and live for him. All her dreams were too small compared to this. Nothing in life could make her as happy as God.

The serpent's lie says, "Your life is all about you." The truth is that God made us to love him and live for him. Our lives will never be right until we live for him. When we try to live for ourselves, it's like trying to put shoes on our hands! It doesn't work. Shoes were made for feet. You were made for God. Life with God is truly happy.

Christmas tells us that Jesus gives us big dreams. Our dreams are too small compared to God's purpose for our life. "No human mind has conceived—the things God has prepared for those who love him!" (1 Corinthians 2 v 9). **We are alive to bring praise to Jesus.**

ENGAGE

⭐ What happens when you believe the lie that "your life is all about you"?

_____

_____

_____

⭐ What gift did God give Mary?

_____

_____

_____

⭐ What purpose does God have for your life, which is bigger than any of your dreams?

_____

_____

_____

⭐ What is it like when we try to live for ourselves instead of for God?

_____

_____

_____

ENTER IN

Father God, you made each of us for a reason. Please teach us what it means to love you and live for you. There are many things we dream about doing. Show us what choices to make so that we live for you. Help us to want to live for you more than for ourselves. Amen.

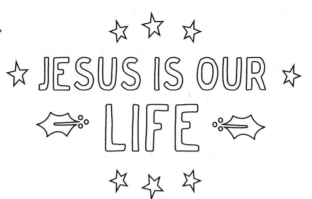

JESUS IS OUR LIFE

FAMILY JOURNALING SPACE

IDEAS: Draw your face looking as happy as Mary was; write the name of your favorite Christmas carol, and sing it together; or something else…

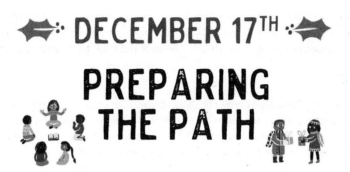

DECEMBER 17TH
PREPARING THE PATH

EXPLORE

Read Luke 1 v 59-60 and 76-79

What will Zechariah's child (John) do to prepare the way for Jesus? (verses 76-77)

_____

_____

_____

What is the result of God's tender mercy? (verses 78-79)

_____

_____

_____

EXPLAIN

Are you ready for Christmas? God promised to help people get ready for Jesus (Isaiah 40 v 1-3). Long ago, people got ready for a king's visit by clearing away stones from the path. Elizabeth and Zechariah's child, John, came to prepare the path for King Jesus. When John grew up he told everyone, "Repent!"— meaning, clear the stones from your heart.

The serpent's lie says, "Our lives are OK just as they are." The truth is, our lives are like a path full of rocks and stones that make us and others fall. When we fall, we feel dirty and run from God. But when we admit to God the wrong things we think, say, and do, we find Jesus is with us, picking us up and making us clean.

Christmas tells us that Jesus forgives our sins and gives us joy. To repent is more than saying "sorry." It is Jesus helping us to love him more than our sin. Jesus helps us to turn around and run to God. **Jesus is the Path to forgiveness and joy.**

ENGAGE

★ A home may look clean until sunshine streams in, showing the dirt and dust. And our lives may look clean until God's light shines in. What "dirt and dust" in your life is God showing you? Will you admit your sin to God? (Adults, talk about what God is showing you, to encourage open sharing.)

★ Who did God send to get people ready for Jesus?

★ Use this space to write a prayer, and ask God to help you see your need for Jesus to pick you up and make you clean.

★ What does it mean to repent?

ENTER IN

Father God, you made a way for us to stop running away from you. Jesus, you are our Path back to God. Most of the time, we don't want to say we're sorry to anyone. Please give us the courage to admit to you the wrong things we think, say, and do. We want to know your forgiveness and joy. Amen.

JESUS FORGIVES SINS

FAMILY JOURNALING SPACE

IDEAS: Draw Elizabeth and Zechariah's baby (John); or write about why being forgiven is so wonderful; or something else...

DECEMBER 18TH
THE REAL JESUS

EXPLORE

Read Luke 2 v 1-7

What names of people and places are in these verses?

_____

_____

_____

Why did Mary and Joseph go to Bethlehem? (verses 4-5)

_____

_____

_____

EXPLAIN

Finally—Christmas came! Baby Jesus was born in Bethlehem. Just as God had promised long before, the King who would rule forever came from King David's home, Bethlehem (Micah 5 v 2). King David's son's son's son's … son is Jesus. Jesus has always lived. Jesus left his home with his Father in heaven to come into our world. And King Jesus will live and rule forever.

The serpent's lie says the story of Jesus is just make-believe. The truth is, Jesus is real. His story is not pretend. Caesar Augustus and Quirinius were real people ruling when Jesus was born. Bethlehem was and is a real place.

Christmas is the real story of God's plan to send Jesus. One day Jesus is coming again, not as a baby but as God's powerful King. At last the world will be as it should be. "The kingdom of the world has become the kingdom of our Lord and of his Messiah, and he will reign for ever and ever" (Revelation 11 v 15). **Jesus is real and he is coming again.**

ENGAGE

⭐ Faith doesn't mean wishing that everything turns out okay. Faith in Jesus is trusting truth. How does knowing that Jesus really lived, died, and came back to life help you know for sure that he is coming again?

_____

_____

⭐ How do we know the story of Jesus is real?

_____

_____

⭐ When Jesus returns, there will be no more death or pain (Revelation 21 v 4). His children will live with him forever in the world as it should be (Revelation 21 v 3). How does this amazing truth change how you want to live today?

_____

_____

_____

⭐ What is God's plan for Jesus?

_____

_____

ENTER IN

Father God, your plan is so much bigger than we ever knew. You put everything in place for Jesus to be born. And you will put it together for his return. When King Jesus comes again, we know we will do whatever he says. Help us to want to do whatever he shows us right now! Amen.

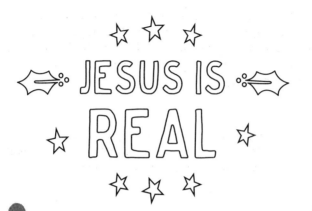

JESUS IS REAL

FAMILY JOURNALING SPACE

IDEAS: Draw the manger Jesus slept in; or list some times when following King Jesus is hard; or something else…

DECEMBER 19TH
THE ANGEL'S MESSAGE FOR ALL

EXPLORE

Read Luke 2 v 8-12

Why were the shepherds in the fields? (verse 8)

_____

_____

_____

Name at least five things the angel told the shepherds. (verses 10-12)

_____

_____

_____

EXPLAIN

Shepherds were the first to hear about Christmas! Shepherds didn't expect to ever hear any good news. Most people stayed away from shepherds. They were smelly and dirty. They didn't wear nice clothes. Shepherds were not usually invited to parties—much less a Christmas party. But God loved the shepherds! He gave them the amazing news, before anyone else, that Jesus was born.

The serpent's lie says that God loves only certain kinds of people. The truth is, God loves people who are rich and poor, good and bad, smart and not so smart. God loves people of every nation, color, and language.

Christmas tells us that Jesus came for all people. You may be young or old, very important or ignored by others. You may know a lot or not yet be able to read. None of these things matter to God. The angels shouted out their joyful message to *all* people: "Today in the town of David a Savior has been born to *you*; he is Christ the Lord." **Jesus came for you.**

ENGAGE

How is God's way of loving people different from the way we usually love people?

Who were the first people God chose to hear that Jesus was born?

How could you reach out to show Jesus's love to someone you think no one else would talk to?

Who did Jesus come for?

ENTER IN

Father God, we're amazed to know about your great love for all people. We admit that we often like people most who look like us and think like we do. Please put your love into our hearts for people who are different than us. And help us to love others as Jesus does. Amen.

JESUS LOVES ALL PEOPLE

FAMILY JOURNALING SPACE

IDEAS: Draw lots of sheep; or write how you feel when you remember that Jesus loves you; or something else…

DECEMBER 20TH
THE BEST
WORDS EVER

EXPLORE

Read Luke 2 v 13-20

What words from God did the angels tell the shepherds? (verse 14)

_____

_____

_____

What did Mary do with the shepherd's words that she knew were from God? (verse 19)

_____

_____

_____

EXPLAIN

The Rescuer was born! The shepherds heard the best words ever! Angels spoke the very words of God to announce the birth of his Son. Today, we hear the best words ever—the very words of God—in his Book, the Bible. God's Book is God speaking to us.

The serpent's lie says, "The Bible is just another book." The truth is, the Bible is not like any other book. God's Book is "sweeter than honey to my mouth!"

(Psalm 119 v 103) When we hear or read the Bible, the Holy Spirit makes God's words sweet to us. In God's Book we hear the sweetest name of all—Jesus.

Christmas tells us that the words about Jesus in God's Book are true. Everything the shepherds saw was just as they had been told. Mary didn't just listen; she "treasured" and "pondered" what she heard. She thought about God's truth long and hard to get all the sweetness out that she could. **God's Book is all about Jesus.**

ENGAGE

How do you know God's Book is different from every other book?

_____

_____

_____

What are the very best words we will ever hear?

_____

_____

Remember when you've tried to make the sweetness last after you ate a piece of candy? Mary wanted to hold the sweet truths of Jesus in her heart forever. What sweet truths about Jesus do you want to hold in your heart?

_____

_____

_____

What makes the Bible different from any other book?

_____

_____

_____

ENTER IN

Father God, we know that we don't love you and your Book as much as we should. Please help us to want to read your Book. Please help us not to love other things more than we love you. Amen.

☆ ☆ ☆
⇒ GOD'S BOOK IS ⇐
ABOUT JESUS
☆ ☆ ☆

FAMILY JOURNALING SPACE

IDEAS: Draw lots of angels in the sky; or write some words of Jesus that you treasure as Mary did; or something else…

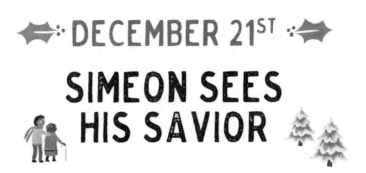

DECEMBER 21ST
SIMEON SEES HIS SAVIOR

EXPLORE

Read Luke 2 v 25-32

What did the Holy Spirit tell Simeon he would see before he died? (verse 26)

What did Simeon know about Jesus that caused him to praise God?
(verses 30-32)

EXPLAIN

God's plan for Christmas included an old man named Simeon. For Simeon's whole life, he had believed God's promises to Abraham. He had prayed for King David's son's son's son's ... son to come and save God's people from the serpent's lies. God gave Simeon a special promise—he would see the Rescuer before he died.

The day had come! When Joseph and Mary brought baby Jesus into the temple, Simeon saw that this baby was the Rescuer. He knew he could die in peace. "For my eyes have seen your salvation," he said. The serpent whispers, "Why do you need to be saved? You are better than most people." The truth is that the terrible lies of the serpent live in every human heart. Even the good things we do are stained by sin.

Christmas tells us that Jesus saves us from sin's punishment and power. Jesus's name means, "He will save us from our sins." Everyone who trusts Jesus is rescued from their sin and welcomed into God's family. **Jesus sets us free from sin to live for him.**

ENGAGE

⭐ If we compare ourselves with others we might say, "Bad people may need Jesus, but I'm pretty good." What is the truth about our sin and Jesus's rescue?

_____

_____

_____

⭐ What special promise did God give to Simeon?

_____

_____

⭐ Have you heard these lies? "Don't worry about sin—God is happy with what you do for him." / "Everybody does some bad things, but when you do, you make up by doing good things." / "Little sins aren't that bad—just tell God you're sorry." What lies does the serpent whisper to you about your sin? What is the truth?

_____

_____

_____

⭐ What did Simeon know when he saw baby Jesus?

_____

_____

ENTER IN

Father God, your kindness is so amazing! Thank you for sending Jesus to save us because we could never save ourselves. Help us see what lies we believe about our sin. And Jesus, please set us free from sin. We want to live for you! Amen.

JESUS SAVES

FAMILY
JOURNALING
SPACE

IDEAS: Draw Simeon's face when he saw the baby Jesus; or write your own prayer; or something else…

✦ DECEMBER 22ND ✦
GOD HEARS US

EXPLORE

Read Luke 2 v 36-39

What did Anna do all day, every day? (verse 37)

How did God show Anna that he had answered her prayers? (verse 38)

EXPLAIN

Anna was part of God's plan for Christmas. Anna was very old. She loved God and believed his promise to send the Rescuer. Her hope, like Eve's, was for the Rescuer to come and crush the serpent's head. She longed for Abraham's son's son's son's … son to come and bless the world. Anna prayed every day that God would send Jesus.

The serpent whispers, "Why pray if God already knows what he is going to do?" The truth is, God uses our prayers to bring about his will, the things he has decided will happen (Isaiah 37 v 21-22, 26). Jesus told us to pray for God's will to be done. He allows us to be part of his work, which will go on forever (Matthew 6 v 9-10). God's children can talk with him like best friends talk.

Christmas tells us we should pray for what God has promised. We know that everything Anna had prayed for was right there in front of her, because her prayers all became thanksgiving and praise. When God's children pray in Jesus's name, we can expect God to hear us. **God hears our prayers because of Jesus.**

ENGAGE

⭐ How do you need God's help today? Will you pray right now for his help? You don't need any special words. Just come to God through faith in Jesus and he will hear you.

⭐ What did Anna pray for every day?

⭐ Who in your life needs to know about God's love? Pray right now for this person and ask God to give you a way to love them this week.

⭐ What is talking to God like for God's children?

ENTER IN

Father God, you are powerful and make everything happen. Thank you for sending Jesus and inviting us to talk to you about anything. We admit that we often live life without praying. Please sound an alarm in our hearts to remind us of how good it is to talk with you. And open our eyes to see what you do! Amen.

☆ ☆ ☆
JESUS'S NAME
OPENS PRAYER
☆ ☆ ☆

FAMILY JOURNALING SPACE

IDEAS: Draw Anna praying; or write how it feels to talk to God like best friends talk; or something else…

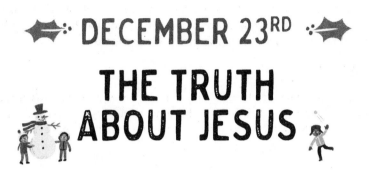

DECEMBER 23RD
THE TRUTH ABOUT JESUS

EXPLORE

Read Matthew 2 v 1-6

The Magi are sometimes called wise men. What did they know about Jesus? (verse 2)

_____

_____

How did people find out where God planned for Jesus to be born? (verses 4-6)

_____

_____

_____

EXPLAIN

The Magi's first Christmas started when they saw a new star shining far away over Israel. A king was born! They were not yet God's children but they wanted to know the truth. They packed their bags and left for Jerusalem. But no one in Jerusalem knew about any baby. Finally, people looked in God's Book. They learned that God's true King would be born in Bethlehem.

The serpent whispers, "What is truth?" The truth is that _Jesus_ is truth. Jesus said, "The reason I was born and came into the world was to testify (be a witness) to the truth" (John 18 v 37). We can see lies better when we know the truth.

Christmas tells us that Jesus is the greatest truth of all. The stars and all of nature show that God is real but they cannot tell us the greatest truth. God's Book tells us that *Jesus* made all stars and trees and creatures (John 1 v 1, 3). When the Magi arrived "they bowed down and worshiped him" (Matthew 2 v 11). They knew Jesus was the King of kings. **Jesus speaks truth and is truth.**

ENGAGE

The Magi left home on a long journey to find the new King. In Jerusalem they finally learned from God's Book the truth about Jesus. How has reading God's Book helped you see the truth, and the lies people believe?

How did the Magi know a king was born?

The Magi worshiped Jesus when they learned he was the true King. What truths about Jesus have you learned that make you want to love him and live for him?

What did the Magi find out about Jesus?

ENTER IN

Father God, Jesus is the truth, so we need to find him. We realize now that we have believed many lies. Please help us to see the truth of Jesus. We want to love him and live for him all our lives. Amen.

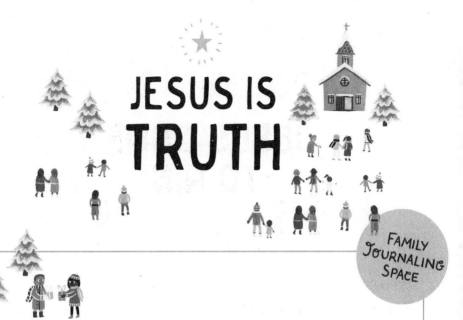

JESUS IS
TRUTH

FAMILY
JOURNALING
SPACE

IDEAS: Draw the Magi following the new star; or list some of the serpent's lies
and write Jesus's truth next to them; or something else…

➤ DECEMBER 24ᵀᴴ ➤
JESUS CAME TO WIN

EXPLORE

Read Matthew 2 v 7-8 and 16-18

What reason did Herod give the Magi for wanting to know more about Jesus? (verse 8)

_____

_____

_____

How did Herod react when he discovered the Magi had outwitted him? (verse 16)

_____

_____

_____

EXPLAIN

Herod didn't like the first Christmas. He was afraid of Jesus. Herod did not want to lose his little kingdom. He could have given his life to God's great King. Instead, Herod tried to kill Jesus. He failed, but his soldiers killed every baby boy around Bethlehem under the age of two.

The serpent whispers, "Why would God allow this to happen?" The truth is, all bad things started in the garden, when Adam and Eve believed the serpent's lie. Sin broke God's perfect world. Now all people are born broken. Herod's awful sin killed the boys. But when God allows something bad to happen, he uses it for good (Romans 8 v 28-32). Jesus's death was wicked, but through the cross he rescues us from sin and death. Now we can be God's children forever.

Christmas tells us that Jesus came to win over sin and death. When Jesus died on the cross, the serpent thought he had won. But Jesus rose to life. He crushed the serpent. Herod and all God's enemies will one day stand before his judgment throne. **Jesus came to right every wrong.**

ENGAGE

How does Jesus's death help us know that God uses the bad things he allows for good?

_____

_____

_____

Who did Herod try to kill?

_____

_____

What hard things that have happened to you, or a friend, will you ask God to use for good?

_____

_____

_____

How did Jesus win over sin and death?

_____

_____

_____

ENTER IN

Father God, you are just and right in all you do. Help us to watch for the good you promise from all things in our lives. Help us to wait and watch for you to work. We want to trust you even when life is hard to understand. Amen.

FAMILY JOURNALING SPACE

IDEAS: Draw Herod looking cross; or write a prayer asking God to help you trust him when hard things happen; or something else…

DECEMBER 25TH
A JESUS CHRISTMAS

EXPLORE

Read John 1 v 1-5 and 9-14 (In these verses Jesus is called "the Word". So, as you read, say "Jesus" each time instead of "the Word".)

Who is the true light that came to shine light into the dark world? (verses 5 and 9-10)

_____

_____

What right does Jesus give to all who believe in him? (verse 12)

_____

_____

EXPLAIN

God's plan for Christmas is Jesus! Jesus is the true Light. He rescues us from darkness. Even the brightest Christmas lights cannot give true light to our minds and hearts. Jesus promises, "Whoever follows me will never walk in darkness, but will have the light of life" (John 8 v 12).

The serpent whispers, "You have enough light to find your way." The truth is, ever since the serpent's lie, darkness has come upon God's perfect world. Adam's and Eve's sin broke the light switch. In the darkness, we cannot see to find our way to become God's children.

Christmas tells us that Jesus is the Light. He fixes the switch and gives us light to trust God and believe his Book. Jesus's light pushes back the darkness. We don't have to believe the serpent's lies any more. We can see that Jesus is the greatest gift of all. "For God, who said, 'Let light shine out of darkness,' made his light shine in our hearts" (2 Corinthians 4 v 6). **Jesus gives light and life.**

ENGAGE

Christmas is all about Jesus. Will you begin the greatest celebration of all by asking Jesus to shine his light into your mind and heart? Will you receive God's gift of Jesus and become a child of God?

Who is the true Light that lights our way to God?

God's children celebrate Christmas all year long by shining Jesus's light into the world. How is Jesus shining out into the dark world through you? In what ways do you want to shine more brightly in the year ahead?

Will you thank God for Jesus—the greatest gift of all? (Lead your child in a short prayer to thank God for sending Jesus to live for us and die for us.)

ENTER IN

Take a few minutes to thank Jesus for his truth.

- Jesus, you are the Light of the world—you have brought me out of darkness.

- Jesus, you are the living Book—you speak to me and help my mind think your truth.

- Jesus, you are the Passover Lamb—you forgive me for believing the serpent's lies and clean my heart.

- Jesus, you are the Tent—you make me at home with the Father so I can walk with him and talk with him.

- Jesus, you are the Manna—you fill me up with your life so that I will enjoy you and glorify you forever.

MERRY CHRISTMAS! This journaling space is for Christmas Day.

FAMILY
JOURNALING
SPACE

IDEAS: Draw your family enjoying Christmas together; or list some things you've learned about Jesus; or something else…

EXTRA SPACE: This journaling space is for any day when you need more room.

FAMILY
JOURNALING
SPACE

EXTRA SPACE: This journaling space is for any day when you need more room.

FAMILY JOURNALING SPACE

EXTRA SPACE: This journaling space is for any day when you need more room.

FAMILY
JOURNALING
SPACE

BAKE THROUGH THE BIBLE

Transform baking with your children into opportunities to teach the Bible!
These Bible overviews for pre-schoolers help parents with young children
to explore the Bible with their child while having lots of fun cooking
together. Written by Susie Bentley-Taylor and Bekah Moore.

thegoodbook.com/bttb
thegoodbook.co.uk/bttb

BIBLE-READING FOR EVERY AGE AND STAGE

Explore
(for adults)

Engage
(for 14+)

Discover
(for 11-13s)

XTB
(for 7-10s)

Table Talk
(for families)

Beginning with God
(for pre-schoolers)

thegoodbook.com/subscriptions
thegoodbook.co.uk/subscriptions

thegoodbook
COMPANY

BIBLICAL | RELEVANT | ACCESSIBLE

At The Good Book Company, we are dedicated to helping Christians and local churches grow. We believe that God's growth process always starts with hearing clearly what he has said to us through his timeless word—the Bible.

Ever since we opened our doors in 1991, we have been striving to produce resources that honor God in the way the Bible is used. We have grown to become an international provider of user-friendly resources to the Christian community, with believers of all backgrounds and denominations using our Bible studies, books, evangelistic resources, DVD-based courses, and training events.

We want to equip ordinary Christians to live for Christ day by day, and churches to grow in their knowledge of God, their love for one another, and the effectiveness of their outreach.

Call us for a discussion of your needs or visit one of our local websites for more information on the resources and services we provide.

Your friends at The Good Book Company

NORTH AMERICA  thegoodbook.com 866 244 2165
UK & EUROPE thegoodbook.co.uk 0333 123 0880
AUSTRALIA thegoodbook.com.au (02) 9564 3555
NEW ZEALAND thegoodbook.co.nz

 WWW.CHRISTIANITYEXPLORED.ORG
Our partner site is a great place for those exploring the Christian faith, with a clear explanation of the good news, powerful testimonies and answers to difficult questions.